INFJ PERSONALITY HANDBOOK

Legal Notice

INFJ Personality Handbook

Understand Yourself as The Rarest Myers-Briggs Personality Type

By: Michelle Hobbs

Contents

Introduction

What is a "personality" exactly? We hear the word a lot, and we probably have a good understanding of the difference between an introvert and extrovert, but there's a lot more to a person. We are complex, but that hasn't stopped researchers and academics from developing systems that try to unlock the depths of personality. The most famous test is the Myers-Briggs Indicator, a popular tool for corporations, therapists, and others.

This test consists of 16 personality types with 4-letter abbreviations, like ISFJ (the most common type) and INFJ (the rarest type and subject of this book). Within these four letters, you learn whether you're an extrovert or an introvert, driven by sensing or intuition, thinking or feeling, and if you tend to judge or perceive. The INFJ personality type, being the rarest, is often misunderstood. This book will shed more light on this personality, whether it describes you or someone you know, and explore how INFJs engage with their careers, friends, significant others, and as parents.

Why does your personality type matter at all? Why should you keep reading? There are three main reasons:

Better understand your purpose

When you learn your type and its makeup, you learn about yourself. If you've ever felt confused about your purpose in life, examining your type can decipher some of your primary motivations. Maybe you are in a job that stresses you out, but you don't know why or what to do about it. Finding your type helps you pinpoint your passions and drive, so you can make a transition into a different role or even a different career that's a better fit.

Improve your relationships

Your personality determines how you interact with the people around you. Are you sensitive and emotional, and crave intimate friendships? Or do you like keeping yourself a bit more closed off and distant from others? Where you fit into the Myers-Briggs Indicator sheds light on your tendencies and challenges, giving you a clearer idea of why your relationships are the way they are. Each personality type has strengths and weaknesses, and understanding them helps you communicate better with your friends, family, and significant other. Your relationships will be stronger and more fulfilling.

Deal with stress better

Life is stressful, whether you're at work or home. Unexpected events occur, plans fall through, and people disappoint us. How we respond flows from our personalities. Knowing your type helps identify the environments and situations that stress you out the most, as well as what you can do to minimize and recover from stress. Self-care has become a more prominent and intentional act in recent years, and your personality type can reveal what works best.

Convinced? This book is the perfect starting point for learning about the INFJ type and its strengths and challenges. After an overview of the history and definitive traits, we'll dig into how the INFJ handles work, friendships, romantic relationships, and family. Whether you're an INFJ or know someone who is, you'll discover fascinating insights and learn how you can improve your life.

Chapter 1: Overview of the Myers-Briggs Indicator

The Myers-Briggs is used in a huge range of fields to give people better insight into themselves and those around them. It can help employers identify the best roles for their employees, improve communication between couples, and enrich a person's understanding of their own behavior. It didn't spring out of thin air, however. It was inspired by Carl Jung, the founder of analytical psychology, and a mother-and-daughter team who combined Jung's work with their own observations.

History

In 1875, Katharine Cook was fortunate to be born into a family that encouraged education for girls as well as boys. After college, she married Lyman James Briggs. In 1897, their daughter Isabel was born, and (Katharine) Briggs began exploring the psychology of raising a child. She educated Isabel at home, allowing her to read and write on whatever topic she wanted. When Isabel grew up and brought home her fiance, Clarence Myers,

Briggs was fascinated by how different he was from her own family. She started researching personality types and developed her own typology theory, which established four "temperaments."

After reading the English translation of Carl Jung's *Psychological Types,* Briggs realized just how far a personality typology could go. Carl Jung's own theories emerged from reconciling his mentor Sigmund Freud and Alfred Adler, who broke from Freud and founded his own ideas about individual psychology and personality. While studying Jung, Briggs saw how much deeper typology went, but it wasn't very useful in a practical sense. Her life's work was just beginning.

In her mother's footsteps

Isabel, now Isabel Briggs Myers, joined her mother's research. Like Briggs, Myers was smart and graduated first in her class at Swarthmore College in 1919. Neither she nor her mother were formerly educated in psychology, but they studied Jung extensively. Myers also worked for Edward N. Hay, the founder of the first successful personnel consulting firm, and from him, learned basic psychometric testing techniques like scoring, validation, and test construction.

Both Briggs and Myers had a firm grasp on personality types by this time, but they wanted to expand the work into a practical form. They began work in earnest on what would become the Indicator during WWII. They hoped that wider knowledge of personality types would help women entering the workforce find jobs best-suited to them. In 1944, they published *The Briggs Myers Type Indicator Handbook*. The names would switch around in 1956.

The Myers-Briggs expands

Briggs died in 1968 at age 93, but Myers didn't slow down. She continuously worked on improving the Myers-Briggs Indicator (MBTI) so it would be as accurate as possible. She also wanted everyday folk to have access to it, not just academics. In 1975, the organization that would become The Myers-Briggs Company published the MBTI for practical applications, and Myers founded the Center for Applications of Psychological Type with Mary McCulley. The nonprofit served as support for MTBI research.

Since then, the MTBI has become a very common and popular tool for business, education, counseling, and more. It's been translated into 30 languages. While once resigned to books and academic discussions, the ideas behind personality are now part of our everyday lives, thanks to the mother-daughter team of Katharine Cook Briggs and Isabel Briggs Myers.

The types

We know how the Myers-Briggs Indicator was created, but what is it exactly? According to the Myers-Briggs Indicator, 16 different personalities exist. They are comprised of combinations of eight possible dichotomies: Extraversion or Introversion, Sensing or Intuition, Thinking or Feeling, and Judging or Perceiving. Every personality can be summarized into a four-letter acronym.

Extraversion (E) or Introversion (I)

If someone's type begins with the Extraversion (E) letter, they are an extrovert. This means they tend to need stimulation from the outside world and they become energized around people and from activities. Introverts, on the other hand, can entertain themselves much more easily, and can become drained by too much external activity and others around them. This doesn't mean extroverts are constantly surrounded by friends while introverts are always alone; the main distinction is that they get their stimulation and energy from different sources.

Sensing (S) or Intuition (N)

The second pair of letters, Sensing vs. iNtuition, refers to how a person absorbs information. Someone with Sensing is most likely pretty practical, and prefers tangible, concrete types of thinking. In a conversation, a Sensing type will probably talk what their kids are up to, what's going on at work, and so on, without analyzing it too deeply. They'll probably want to get a board game going as opposed to sitting around and just talking. If the news is on, an S-type is more likely to listen to whatever the journalists are saying without questioning it.

An iNtuitive, however, likes abstract, imaginative thinking. They are going to be talking about God, politics, philosophy, and more. They analyze everything and make connections that aren't obvious. N-types aren't interested in day-to-day routines, so at a party, it wouldn't be unusual to see an N lost in conversation with the last guest while their spouse tries to clean up. Turn on the news for a while, and an N-type will have to think about everything they hear, measuring it against their own internal journalist, before deciding what they believe.

Thinking (T) or Feeling (F)

How do you make decisions? Do you value logic and rational thought over your gut? Or do you believe the heart is better at important choices? Thinking types prioritize logic and reason over emotion, which can make them more impartial and unbiased. However, leading with logic can often result in seeming callous and hurting others' feelings.

Interestingly enough, more men are T-types than women, which could be because of how society perceives emotional men as weak. Feeling types weigh emotions more heavily in their decisions, including the emotions of others. In general, they are more compassionate.

Judging (J) or Perceiving (P)

This last pair of letters is a bit trickier to understand than the others. In general, however, whether someone is a J or a P-type can be deciphered by their outward responses to the world. It can actually be hard to figure out for yourself if you're a J or a P; other people who see your behavior might be better at identifying your type.

What's odd about this last letter is that everyone is both a J and a P. If you are a J on the outside, you are a P on the inside, and vice versa. This is because others can't see the function a person naturally leads with; that first letter is always an inwardly-directed function, while the last letter describes what the world sees.

A Judging type is more likely to be very decisive. Once you've made a call, you want to stick with it. You don't like loose ends or a lack of structure. You like an organized house and workspace and often find it hard to focus if things are out of place. That said, J-types can be just as messy as P-types; it doesn't seem to matter. P-types are more adaptable and easy-going, however, even in the face of clutter. They're comfortable with the open-ended and go-with-the-flow structures. They are more likely to change their opinions based on outside ideas and worldviews.

But wait, there's more

Personality can be broken down even further. The Sensing/Intuition and Thinking/Feeling functions can be classified as either "introverted" or "extraverted," which is a bit confusing since we already have Extraversion and Introversion as functions on their own. Those E/I letters are actually determined by looking at the introverted/extraverted classifications and how they manifest in a person's personality.

What the classifications designate is whether or not the function it's describing is directed inwardly or outwardly. When someone has an introverted feeling, it means it isn't manifesting to the world around them; others can't see it. When someone has extraverted Feeling, however, (the INFJ-type has this) it's obvious because the person is known for their compassion, kindness, and interest in other people.

You can break the functions down again into whether or not they're judging or perceiving. The Thinking (both introverted and extraverted) and Feeling (both introverted and extraverted) functions are Judging, while Sensing and Intuition in both their introverted and extraverted forms are Perceiving. What does this mean? Judging functions are about control, organization, and decision-making. Perceiving is about absorbing new information and making observations. Here's a chart from Dr. A. J. Drenth over at Personality Junkie that can help you visualize how types are organized:

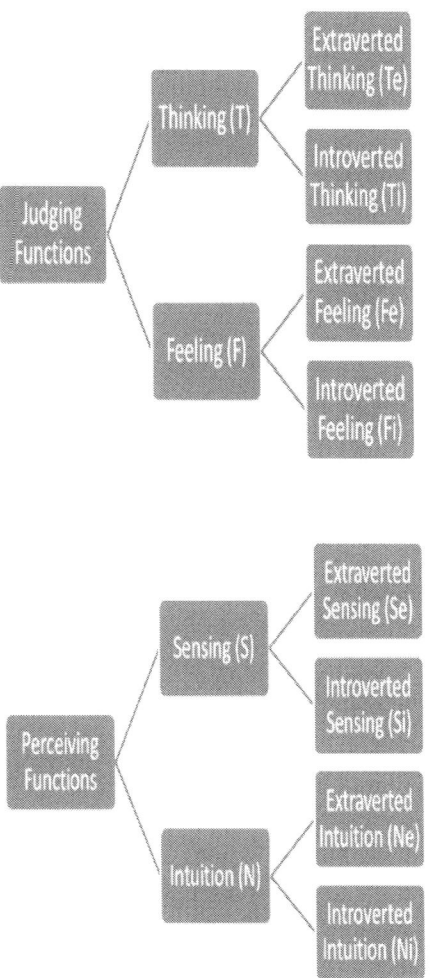

Reflections/discussion questions

- If you weren't familiar with the Myers-Briggs Indicator before, what aspect of it sticks out most to you? Why?
- If you aren't an INFJ, do you have a guess as to what personality type you might be?
- If you are familiar with the Myers-Briggs and know your type, do you agree or disagree with any aspects of it?

Chapter 2: Unraveling the INFJ Personality

As you learned, every personality can be classified into one of 16 combinations. The INFJ type is the rarest; research shows it makes up only 1-3% of the population. The INFJ is Introverted, iNtuitive, Feeling, and Judging. What does this mean?

Compassion, purpose, and creativity

INFJs are naturally altruistic and concerned about the feelings of others. As a J-type, they show the world their Feeling function. Their understanding of the people around them can sometimes make them appear extroverted because they are so interested in others, but INFJs are textbook introverts. They need alone time to recharge, and prefer small groups where they can talk one-on-one to others. Large crowds and noise can be overwhelming. Even in an ideal setting, it often takes time for an INFJ to feel really connected to another person. While others may consider an INFJ a close friend, the INFJ might be hesitant to share too much of their emotions.

Meaningful goals are very important to INFJs. They are principled and always seek deeper meaning in everything around them, including themselves. When it comes to problem-solving and creative thinking, INFJs excel. They are adaptable because they don't like conflict, which makes them receptive to creative solutions. Tedious routines are not interesting to INFJS; they prefer more independence, where they can exercise their own ideas and improve on how things are done. They are generally very productive workers and organize information very well.

The Dominant, Auxiliary, Tertiary, and Inferior hierarchy

In her work with typology, Isabel Myers believed that the four letters in each personality type formed a hierarchy. This means that people lean more into certain aspects of their type than others, though with time and intentional action, the weaker functions can become stronger. Every type has a Dominant, Auxiliary, Tertiary, and Inferior function. The Dominant function represents where the person is most comfortable, while the Inferior is essentially their greatest weakness. Here's how the hierarchy breaks down for the INFJ:

Dominant: Introverted intuition (Ni)

INFJs are primarily driven by their Intuition function, and it's introverted. That's why INFJ begins with "I." What makes the INFJ's Ni function especially unique is that it allows the person to access their intuition at a higher level than most. This can make them almost appear psychic. INFJs value their own perspectives above outside ones, since they've done so much inner work to get to a place of understanding. Another feature of the Ni is the ability to reconcile opposites through synthesizing information. INFJs are very fond of symbols and images, so they tend to employ those while processing and reaching a conclusion.

Auxiliary: Extraverted feeling (Fe)

Thanks to their Feeling, INFJs are very good at interpreting emotional expressions and body language. It's extraverted, which makes them appear more social than a traditional introvert, but they are still definitely introverted. The INFJ's extraverted Feeling function is abbreviated as "Fe." INFJs care very deeply about positivity and harmony in their environment. This makes them polite, affable, and compassionate. However, because of their desire to avoid conflict, an INFJ's Ni and Fe sometimes clash. For example, if they see something going on in a group that they don't agree with, the Ni perks up. At the same time, the Fe wants to keep everything calm and agreeable, so the INFJ must choose which trait to engage with. If they decide to maintain the peace, an INFJ will often harbor inward guilt about betraying the greater good.

Tertiary: Introverted thinking (Ti)

When you start digging into the hierarchy of personalities, you'll see letters and functions that don't show up in the abbreviation, but they're still a part of the person's personality. However, since this is a tertiary function, it's much weaker. An INFJ's Thinking is focused inwardly and concerned with what info was gathered from the Fe. Their emotional intelligence is much stronger than their logic, so it's a temptation to ignore the more reasonable conclusion. Sometimes, those functions can clash. INFJs may have to choose which function to trust and over time, they can achieve a healthy balance.

Inferior: Extroverted sensing (Se)

Considering extraverted Sensing is the weakest function for an INFJ, it makes sense that it doesn't appear among those four letters. As the Inferior, it means an INFJ is the least comfortable with it and has difficulty accessing it. This translates into overstimulation around loud noises and activity, and a tendency to lose sense of details, especially physical ones. An INFJ can get so lost in thought and their inward impressions of the environment and people, they miss specifics. The physical world and its stimuli (new sights, sounds, other experiences) are uncomfortable to an INFJ, even scary. This weakness manifests at work and in relationships, so we'll explore how to deal with related stress in the relevant chapters.

Famous INFJs

INFJs may be rare, but there's no shortage of famous examples. Carl Jung himself, the inspiration for the Myers-Briggs, is one of them. Many of them are artistic, like songwriters, writers, and actors, though there are a handful of political powerhouses that match the INFJ criteria as well. As a note, this list is not based on actual test results, but on observations of the person's personality and behavior. You can find more examples on sites like the Personality Club.

Carl Jung
Jane Goodall
Adolf Hitler
Eleanor Roosevelt
Mahatma Gandhi
Carrie Fisher
Tilda Swinton
Nicole Kidman
Leonard Cohen
Taylor Swift
Nathaniel Hawthorne
J.K. Rowling

Reflections/discussion questions

- When do you feel keenly aware that you're more intuitive than others around you? Reflect on some of those experiences and how they make you feel.
- When do you feel most overwhelmed by external stimuli? What emotions do you feel?
- Think about your heroes and role models. How many of them do you believe are INFJS?

Chapter 3: The INFJ At Work

In general, an INFJ is a very creative and independent-minded worker. This makes them a good fit for the arts and science, which both call for outside-the-box thinking and problem-solving. They are also drawn to non-profits and careers with a focus on service, which appeals to their natural compassion. It's no wonder that two of their shorthand titles are "The Advocate" and "The Counselor."

INFJs like being given a task and then left to it. They don't enjoy tedious routines, like the kind found in accounting or data-input jobs. You'll frequently find INFJs in positions where they are their own boss. Because of their desire for peace and harmony, they get stressed when conflict arises. This makes them uncomfortable in situations where they need to give or receive constructive criticism. INFJs tend to take things too personally. That's the INFJ at work in a nutshell. Now, let's get into their strengths and weaknesses in more depth.

Strengths

Because of their rarity, it's possible for companies to have only a handful or so or no INFJs at all on their staff. This would be unfortunate because of what an INFJ can bring the table. They are driven, strategic, independent, compassionate, and inspiring.

Principled strategists

INFJs are hardworking, loyal, and principled. The values of a company are very important to an INFJ, which is why you're unlikely to find them working for corporations with sketchy business dealings or in fields where profit is the top priority. INFJs focus on what's best for the company and for the people they work with, which ensures a healthy balance of hard work and boosted morale. When driven by a cause they believe in, INFJs are excellent strategists and capable of solving complex problems when given the time and space they need. They're usually very good at organizing information and communicating their findings.

Independently-motivated

If you prefer to work on a project in a quiet place by yourself than in a busy office because it lets you explore your ideas in an organized, effective manner, you are probably an INFJ or at least share traits with this type. Being independently-motivated is a great asset to just about any company; INFJs don't need a lot of prompting beyond being allowed to work on something they care about. They enjoy the process of creative problem-solving and can be trusted to tackle a good challenge head-on. After careful thought, an INFJ will stick to a decision and follow through.

Compassionate team players

Because INFJs are so in-tune with what's going on with the people around them, they're great additions to any team project. They can quickly identify a person's strengths and encourage them to achieve their best potential. More concerned with the feelings of others than with being right, an INFJ is a great listener. Using their intuitive abilities and analyzing skills, they are able to synthesize seemingly opposing ideas into something cohesive, which is extremely valuable. If a group is having trouble coming together for whatever reason, you as an INFJ can be the stabilizing force and voice of unity.

<u>Inspiring leaders</u>

When an INFJ is the boss, they are excellent at inspiring and encouraging others towards a shared vision. They aren't just all talk, however; an INFJ boss will most likely be in the trenches right alongside their subordinates because they truly believe in the mission. This willingness to put in the hard work endears others to the INFJ leader and strengthens the team's purpose. Because of their intuition and sensitivity to others' feelings, an INFJ leader is very approachable and compassionate.

Challenges

Every personality type has its challenges, especially at work where there's often a lot going on. INFJs have very specific needs (freedom to be creative, core values they can get behind, etc) that not every workplace can meet, and their emotional sensitivity can cause friction with colleagues.

Dealing with rules, regulations, and routine

INFJs don't like rigid hierarchies, micro-managers, or projects without a purpose. If they aren't allowed to think creatively about problems, but are forced to do things according to the status quo, they'll be very unhappy. Hovering managers with strict rules also make INFJs uncomfortable. If their boss critiques their work using frequent check-ins, an INFJ will get stressed. They want to be allowed to do their own thing and get the project done *their way*. They believe they have the best tools and ideas to be effective, and when they are forced on a different path, it's very difficult. INFJs want to break the mold, not fit into it.

Rules and tedious routines are also challenging for INFJs because they lose the sense of *why*. They continuously come back to the meaning of their work, the higher goal. If it's bogged down by bureaucracy and administrative issues, an INFJ becomes disheartened. They like having the greater purpose front-and-center and are often unable to succeed in careers with lots of red tape masking it.

Making tough decisions

At work, hard decisions often need to be made. Reassigning roles on a team, offering constructive criticism, or even firing someone are not-so-rare events. Depending on the type of job, they might even be a regular occurence. INFJs hate this type of decision-making. They will avoid confrontational conversations or discussions where hard news must be delivered. When giving feedback or delivering bad news about a project or the company's future, they'll try to paint the situation in the best light possible, often miscommunicating the full message. As a leader, this trait can have disastrous results. The success of a project or an entire company could be in jeopardy if the INFJ leader can't force themselves to take on the hard tasks.

Receiving constructive criticism

INFJs really dislike being the recipient of hard truths as much as they dislike being the bearer. They tend to take things too personally and can become bristly and defensive. For people who don't like conflict, they can react surprisingly strongly to being questioned or critiqued, and it isn't a good look in the workplace.

What about criticism that isn't constructive? What about harassment and bullying? INFJs are especially vulnerable. While they often respond sharply to feedback, many remain calm in service of keeping the peace, while they stew inside. However, when the criticism is actually a personal attack or even abusive, an INFJ might stay quiet because they are hesitant to make a stand. They want to give a person the benefit of the doubt, and this can led to a work environment that's toxic for everyone.

Managing fast and unorganized information

INFJs like to take their time processing information. Thanks to their excellent intuitive skills and ability to analyze, they notice more than most people, and need time to process it all. At work, however, information can come on hard and fast, and it isn't always organized. An INFJ feels the need to pause, organize everything, and then make a decision, but not every workplace provides enough time. An environment that's all about speed would terrify an INFJ. Imagine a place like the stock exchange that's fast-paced, loud, and chaotic. As an INFJ, that's your worst nightmare.

<u>Handling unexpected events</u>

INFJs may be creative, but they are not spontaneous. They use their intuition and feeling skills to craft a plan, and they like to stick to it. However, at work, unexpected changes often pop up. Project deadlines get moved, new team members come in, and so on. An INFJ will naturally want to resist these changes and maintain course. They can get overwhelmed if changes start piling up quickly and dig their heels in even more. Their stubborness can lead to power struggles within a team and the loss of productivity. Tempers might flare, which causes even more stress for the INFJ.

How INFJs can deal with workplace stress

Based on the challenges we just discussed, INFJs experience different pressures at work.

You might get overwhelmed with information during a project with a quick turn-around, or anxious about an assessment. Perhaps you need to deal with an unproductive team member on a project you're leading, and you feel sick at the thought of criticising them. Whatever job you're in, there will be stress. It's impossible to find a perfect job where everything always goes your way, so how do you deal with the stress as an INFJ?

Give your brain a break

Over-extending your introverted intuition function at work leads to burnout. You'll be exhausted and ineffective. Give yourself breaks, so you can recharge. Spending some time in a quiet place, without working on anything, is really good for INFJs. Try meditation or something physical, like yoga, jogging, or taking a stroll. Spend time looking at nature and fostering your weakest function, extraverted sensing. It will take you out of your own head for a while.

Vent to someone outside of work about problems

INFJs have extraverted Feeling, but they often can't express that at work, because it wouldn't be appropriate to complain to colleagues or a boss about everything. Instead, an INFJ should have a trusted friend, other loved one, or even a therapist who they feel comfortable venting to. This can be difficult because INFJs are guarded and even possessive of their emotions. They also don't like to focus too much on themselves for very long. If you've ever vented to a friend and then felt guilty about complaining, you know this feeling well. However, INFJs need some kind of outward expression of work frustrations. The alternative is an internal simmer of negative feelings, which can lead to bitterness and even worse guilt.

Practice handling criticism in a healthy way

Constructive criticism and feedback is just part of a job. INFJs really dislike it, but they can get better at receiving it. The first step is to assume that everyone has good intentions when they offer you feedback. They want to help you improve, so you can succeed. If they didn't care or wanted you to fail, they would stay silent.

The other important thing to remember is that you aren't being personally attacked. Criticism of your work is not about who you are as a person. You don't have to defend yourself and make excuses. Accept that everyone (and that includes you) makes mistakes. That's how you learn. Receiving feedback is the only way you'll know what your mistakes are, so you don't end up repeating them.

Accept that you can't control everything

INFJs like having an idea of what's going to happen. They make a decision and they want to see it through. However, things can change, and that bothers INFJs. It can be very stressful to feel out of control, especially if you've laid out your plans and were anticipating a certain result. To better manage the resulting stress, learn to accept that you can't control everything. Life will not stick to the schedule you planned, and that's okay. You can still make decisions and plans, but when something at work changes, learn to tweak them. Remember the big picture and let go of everything else. This will be a lifelong process, but you'll get better at it as time goes on, and you'll have significantly less stress.

Best careers for INFJs

Given the strengths and weaknesses of the INFJ personality type, what jobs are the best fit? What jobs should be avoided? Every INFJ is a little bit different with unique passions and motives, but given what we know about their functions, it's possible to generalize what careers are a good match and which are not. Here's a list of the best jobs for INFJs according to ZipRecruiter:

Psychologist

The father of personality tests, Carl Jung, was both a psychologist and an INFJ. The INFJ traits are a perfect fit for the field, which involves creative problem-solving, analyzing human minds and behaviors, and more. In terms of what specific area of psychology (research, private practice, etc) is best, it depends on the individual and what they're most passionate about.

Therapist

Like psychologists, therapists spend a lot of time exploring the human mind, but with counseling, there's a much more explicitly compassionate reason. Therapists act as guides for those wanting to improve themselves, whether it's recovering from trauma, learning to manage a mental illness, or communicating better with others. An INFJ would be really good at reading clients through their words, expressions, and body language. Best of all, INFJs are naturally empathetic, which is essential for a good therapist.

Artist (writer, musician, designer)

If it involves something creative like writing, painting, or songwriting, an INFJ would probably enjoy it as a career. These fields involve a lot of inward thinking and analysis, imagination, and creative problem-solving. An INFJ can create their own world and communicate it very effectively. There is a lot of criticism associated with being an artist, however, which can be tough for an INFJ. However, once they've learned how to manage their feelings about critiques, they still love their work. In the words of one famous INFJ (Taylor Swift), sometimes you just have to "shake it off."

Scientist

While artist and scientist may seem like opposite sides of the spectrum, they're actually pretty similar in their essences. Like an artist, a scientist must think outside-the-box and exercise creative problem-solving. Whether it's in a lab or while solving a math equation, a speedy finish is not the priority; the journey is what's important. There's also often a higher goal in mind when it comes to the sciences, like curing a disease. An INFJ will appreciate just how meaningful their work is and stay excited and inspired.

Humanitarian

It's very common to see INFJs working for nonprofits and advocacy groups. They are driven by their core beliefs and when they find a workplace with colleagues that believe the same thing, there's no stopping them. INFJs can be very effective and inspiring, while also excelling at the more complex challenges that nonprofits face. One of the great humanitarians of all time, Eleanor Roosevelt, was an INFJ.

Jobs that aren't an ideal fit

Given an INFJ's traits, there are certain jobs that are best avoided. Every person is different, however, and there are certainly INFJs who enjoy success in careers that seem to run counter their personality. In general, however, these are the jobs that aren't the best fit if you're an INFJ:

Sales

In the corporate world of sales, profit is the top priority. It's all about how many clients you can get in terms of status and your own financial gain. Sales are usually commission-based, which can be extremely stressful for an INFJ if they don't truly believe in what they're selling. They also don't like coming across as aggressive or pushy to potential customers, which is part of the risk of sales. Because of this, the INFJ's boss might see them as timid and give lots of feedback, which INFJs do not like. Unless the INFJ really believes in whatever they're selling and is able to let go of the numbers aspect of the job, sales is just too consistently stressful for this personality.

Customer service

No one goes to customer service because they want to tell a company how great they are. More often than not, they want to complain about something, and that kind of confrontation is extremely uncomfortable to an INFJ. They just want everyone to be happy, and that isn't always possible with customer service. More companies would probably benefit from the very compassionate nature of an INFJ, but the INFJ themself, dealing with frustrated or angry customers all day would be troubling. On top of that, if you didn't agree with the company's policies regarding perturbed clients, you'd have a very hard time being a representative.

Military

The military is all about rules and regulation. That's the one thing every soldier needs to learn: follow the rules. Creative problem-solving and doing things at your own pace are not a part of this career *at all.* For an INFJ, it would be agony, especially if they see or experience something that goes against their core values. The military can be an ethically-messy place, and questioning why something is being done is not welcomed. If you're an INFJ and considering entering the military, you might want to rethink it. At the very least, reflect on why you want this career. Be prepared to endure an institute that will constantly grate against your true nature.

Finance/clerical work

There's a lot of busy work in finance or clerical jobs, and not much room for creativity. When it comes to math and certain types of data, there's usually just one right way to do it. That can be soul-draining for an INFJ yearning to think outside-the-box. The routine gets old very quickly and and INFJs will start to get existential and wonder about their life's meaning.

<u>Jobs with lots of sensory overload
(construction, mechanic)</u>

Extraverted sensing is the weakest function for
an INFJ, so jobs with lots of noise and
stimulation are overwhelming. This includes
construction or jobs at auto shops, where
there's a lot of sound, smells, and other sensory
activity. An INFJ will feel very uncomfortable
and always want to seek out a quiet place, but
depending on the job, this won't be possible
without stopping everything. They'll have a lot
of trouble focusing and being productive, and
the job just won't be rewarding.

Reflections/discussion questions

- If you could design your ideal job, what
  would it be?
- Do you feel like you're in a job that gives
  you a purpose or are you just counting
  the days until retirement?
- What are some ways you deal with
  workplace stress? Can you think of any
  more that might help?

Chapter 4: The INFJ as Friend and Family Member

What is friendship and family life like for the INFJ? They are most likely the warm, calming, and emotional center of the group. People feel comfortable and *seen* with the INFJ, thanks to the INFJ's seemingly uncanny ability to read facial expressions, body language, and what's between peoples' words. Even people who don't know them well are drawn to the INFJ. Since INFJs value harmony, they seek out reconciliation in conflict, and probably won't be the person at the party bringing up politics. Even if something is said that contradicts their personal values, they are likely to stay quiet in order to maintain the peace. Within family groups, the INFJ is the one who tries to get people to come back together if there's been a divide.

While the INFJ naturally inspires openness in others, they are usually guarded with their own emotions. They prefer to let others spill their guts and are very careful about who they share with. They value long-term relationships built on one-on-one conversations, and are often very uncomfortable and quiet in large groups. Get them alone, however, and INFJs can be very talkative. If they feel safe with the person, they'll show more vulnerability. They may not have a ton of close friendships, but the ones they do have are very important, and the INFJ takes great care in nurturing them.

Strengths

The INFJ is a great friend to everyone who has the privilege of knowing them, and there are specific reasons why. They invest in relationships and never break a person's trust. They are encouragers and always there when someone needs a good cry. If you're an INFJ, you're always willing to step in the role of the peacemaker and make compromises to protect a relationship. Let's dig into these strengths a bit more:

Loyal and trustworthy

INFJs are not "friends of the road" if they can help it. When they connect with a person, they put a lot of energy into the relationship. They are completely present in every conversation and interaction, so the person knows they can rely on the INFJ. In family groups, the INFJ is the one their siblings go to for advice because they know the INFJ will always be there with a cup of something warm and a shoulder to cry on. Both friends and family can trust the INFJ to not reveal anything told in confidence. The INFJ is keenly aware of how that betrayal would feel and they care too much about their friends and families' feelings to inflict that pain.

Encouraging and compassionate

Thanks to their extraverted feeling function, INFJs are very encouraging and compassionate in their friendships. If someone is ever feeling down and insecure, the INFJ will be able to tell even if no words are spoken, and they'll jump to action. When a friend expresses difficult feelings, the INFJ is a supportive presence. They can pick up when someone wants advice and when they just want to vent. Friends and family don't need to worry about being judged or criticized for their feelings. After talking to an INFJ, people feel loved, encouraged, and even inspired.

Always willing to make peace

INFJs are very protective of their relationships with friends and family. You shield them from conflict and when storms start brewing, you'll be the one to guide the ship back to the shore. INFJs prioritize relationships over just about anything, so they're willing to "agree to disagree" and move past areas of division. They don't understand why something petty (according to each individual INFJ's definition) should tear a friendship apart. If there's tension in a conversation, the INFJ will always want to end on a high note and reassure their friend (and get reassurance back) that everything is good. As an INFJ, you never let the sun go down on your (or anyone else's) anger. Your friends and family rarely feel like they've been left out in the cold emotionally after a conflict.

Challenges

Because of their sensitivity and dislike of conflict, INFJs have challenges in friendships. You might often feel hurt by the actions and words of others, and misunderstood. This can make it hard to trust and find connections. On top of that, INFJs often have trouble understanding that not everyone is as intuitive or in touch with the emotional world as they are. INFJs usually have high expectations. With the connections and relationships they do possess, they have a tendency to avoid conflict even when they're being railroaded by stronger, less compassionate personalities.

<u>Can be closed-off emotionally</u>

Do you find it hard to open up emotionally? Does vulnerability scare you? If so, you're dealing with a classic INFJ challenge. While INFJs seek out emotionally-charged friendships, they are very private about their own feelings. This creates an inward clash. You want close relationships, but are too cautious to give the vulnerability needed to build them. You like it when others are vulnerable with you, and they usually are, but being vulnerable yourself can be very hard. This limits the depth of relationships with friends and family, leaving you unfulfilled.

Can have unrealistic expectations for relationships

Reading other people comes so naturally for an INFJ, they often believe that everyone has the same ability. Have you ever had a bad day and then felt upset that your friend didn't ask you what was wrong? Sure, you didn't say anything, but they should have noticed your body language and facial expressions, right? INFJs expect their friends and family to read them like the INFJ reads them. This inevitably leads to disappointment.

INFJs also have high expectations about how much effort should go into a friendship. They consistently put the feelings of others before their own and pour a lot of energy into relationships, but when that isn't reciprocated equally, they feel undervalued, even rejected. When you send a text and your friend doesn't reply all day, do you ever think, "They must think I'm annoying. They don't want to be friends anymore?" If so, you're dealing with a classic "high-expectations" dilemma.

Can be passive when trying to avoid conflict

INFJs just want everyone to be happy. They often feel uncomfortable by something as harmless as a friendly debate about dogs versus cats. Once a conflict escalates into something more serious, INFJs will be tempted to surrender, even if means allowing someone to bully them. They're willing to take an emotional beating if it means there will be peace afterwards. This is especially common among family, because your family is much harder to avoid than your friends.

However, not standing up for yourself can have painful consequences. You might harbor your bitterness instead of expressing it, and then one day, it gets to be too much and you blow up. Now you have a *real* conflict on your hands and there may not be anything you can do to fix it. An INFJ will feel agonizing guilt and blame themselves for the whole mess. The other possibility is that you never stand up for yourself, and are gradually broken down into a person who is miserable and insecure. You just keep being passive and it spreads to every other relationship. Neither of these paths are healthy or fulfilling.

<u>Can ignore their own emotional needs</u>

INFJs are so emotionally-savvy and kind, people often treat them like therapists. INFJs don't like saying no to people, which leads to everyone in their life coming to them for comfort and advice. Setting boundaries is very hard, because INFJs don't want anyone to feel like they're being rejected or abandoned. If this sounds like you, you're dealing with the last most common challenge for an INFJ. It's all too easy to get so consumed with the feelings of others that you forget to take care of your own. You'll become exhausted and bottled up, and maybe even bitter that it seems like no one is there for you. Emotional burnout and even breakdowns are not rare for INFJs.

How INFJs can improve friend and family relationships

How do you address the problems that the above challenges tend to create? As an INFJ, you don't like criticism, but don't think of the following advice as a scolding. Think of it as building on your existing strengths in unexpected ways. These are tools that will help your friendships thrive and flourish.

Redefine your expectations

Redefining expectations for your friendships and relationships with family is arguably the best thing you can do to improve them. As an INFJ, reading people comes naturally, and you put a lot of energy into nurturing these relationships based on what you know. Other personalities, however, express their love differently and aren't as intuitive about emotions and needs. Maybe they aren't good about answering texts right away, but when you see them in person, they are very focused on your time together.

Instead of feeling like a friend isn't consistent or reliable, realize that they simply prioritize the in-person aspect of a friendship. Sure, *you* always text back right away and get frustrated when they don't do the same for you, but a person doesn't need to meet all your expectations to be a good friend. Exercise your compassionate and understanding skills to give your friend grace. Turn your criticism of your friend around on yourself and take a good look at your expectation. You might be asking for something they aren't able to give.

Open up a bit more

If you're feeling unfulfilled in your relationships and want to deepen them, consider becoming more vulnerable. Being open encourages openness in the other person; trust goes both way. Strong friendships are made when both people feel trusted. Vulnerability can be a bit scary, especially if you've been burned before, so it's okay to be careful. Take it slow with new friendships. You don't have to spill your guts about your deepest, darkest secrets to be open. Just be aware of moments when you can show your true self - admit an embarrassing moment, give your opinion about a movie you saw recently, or share when you're feeling anxious about something.

People often think of INFJs as unshakeable pillars of emotional strength because they don't like to show weakness. While that prompts many people to go INFJs for advice, it can lead a relationship where the INFJ is treated like a counselor, not a friend. When you're vulnerable, others will see you as a real human being. You'll be trustworthy and credible because you've lived through good and bad experiences. The friendship will be more fulfilling for both you.

Have friends you can just have fun with

Not every relationship needs to be super deep. This goes along with redefining your expectations, and by accepting that some friends will just be the kind you go to happy hour with, you won't be asking for something they can't give. Having friends that are just fun is really good for an INFJ. You might be so locked in your head all the time that you forget to just enjoy yourself. You will need friends you can have deep conversations with, but sometimes, you need to relax. A friend with a very different personality type can encourage you to exercise parts of your identity that are often ignored, like extraverted sensing. They will also not expect your full focused emotional attention, like another INFJ might. You can just let go and go with the flow.

Set boundaries

As an INFJ, you want to help everyone. You see their emotional cracks and feel the need to heal them. The world needs more compassion like this, but not everyone who crosses your path will treat you fairly. Too often, INFJs are taken advantage of, intentionally and unintentionally. INFJs tend to attract broken people, and sometimes, that brokenness can be destructive. You might know when a friendship is toxic, but don't want to hurt the person by stepping back. In the long run, allowing someone to exploit you damages both people.

Learn to set boundaries with your friends and family members. It is not your job to fix them. If they are calling you at all hours of the day and night, don't always drop everything to talk them through a problem. If their emotional venting turns on you and they start using you as a soundboard for their negativity, learn to distance yourself. Boundaries can be challenging, especially with family, but they're so necessary. A good therapist can help you figure out how to set emotional perimeters that don't generate unnecessary conflict, if you're anxious about the process.

Focus on yourself a bit more

Setting boundaries is part of self-care, which is something INFJs often have trouble remembering. They're so concerned with the feelings of others and keeping the peace that they ignore their own emotional needs. Do you frequently do activities you don't really like just because others want to? Or maybe you call your mom every day because she expects it, but her tendency to critique your life is draining and leaves you feeling insecure? When you find yourself always fatigued emotionally (and even physically), your selflessness has most likely crossed a line. You need some self-care.

What is self-care? It's anything that recharges and inspires you. That might be taking time every morning to journal or take a jog. Instead of asking a friend what they want to do, suggest an activity that you really enjoy. When you've had a long work week, stay in alone on Friday night with a movie, even though your sister wants to hang out. Call a trusted friend and this time, you vent about something. Taking care of yourself is not selfish. It's actually the opposite, because when you give so much of yourself that there's nothing left, what can you give to others?

Friends with or related to an INFJ? Here's what you can do

If you aren't an INFJ, but you're pretty sure you know one, how can you respond to their strengths and needs to improve the friendship? There are four things you can do:

Affirm the relationship

INFJs can feel insecure about where they stand with friends and family. They often feel neglected because others don't put as much energy in the relationship as they would like, and it leaves them feeling like they aren't a priority. This can come across as neediness, and unfortunately, it sometimes drives people away. If you are friends with an INFJ, realize that they need affirmation about what you mean to them. The gestures don't have to be big; send a text after a conversation that says something like, "Thanks for always being there for me, it means a lot," or "You're such a great friend for listening to me, I really appreciate it." This tells the INFJ that their hard work is not going unnoticed.

Other ideas for affirmation include gifts, spending time together where you commit to asking the INFJs how they are and not vice versa, and responding to texts/emails/phone calls within a reasonable time frame. Anything you do to show the INFJ that their friendship is important will make them happy.

<u>Be real</u>

INFJs desire deep relationships. They aren't interested in "small talk." Most are perfectly capable of keeping things light and breezy, but for them to feel like a friendship is real, they want more personal, deep connections. As the friend of an INFJ, it's very important to remember this, and to allow conversations to drift into deeper waters. Engage with the INFJ on topics like philosophy, the meaning of life, and emotional struggles. It may seem odd to spend an hour talking about the feminism of modern rom-coms, but the INFJ will leave the conversation feeling more connected to you. They'll feel appreciated.

While we're on the subject of keeping it real, you should also keep it honest with your INFJ friends and family. INFJs can read people better than most personality types. They pick up on small expressions, body language, and vocal tone. If you aren't being honest with them, they probably know. They'll believe you don't trust them, and that's incredibly painful for an INFJ. You should only share what you're comfortable with, of course, but don't try to pretend everything is fine. You should at least tell the INFJ that yes, something is going on, but you don't want to talk about it yet. It may still sting the INFJ a bit, but that's their problem, and they'll feel a lot better than if you just lie.

Give the INFJ some space

INFJs love people, but because they are introverts, they get drained and need time alone. If they are close enough with someone like a sibling, they are sometimes able to "recharge" while hanging out one-on-one, but it's usually if they don't feel the need to talk. For example, a recharge might look like watching a movie at home, surrounded by snacks, or an evening where you two both bury your noses in a book. In general, however, an INFJ will need time totally alone. If they don't get that time, they can become withdrawn. It may even look like they're angry with you. They aren't.

The best thing you can do in these situations is let the INFJ have their alone time. If you know the INFJ has been spending a lot of time with people, don't ask them to hang out right away. Give them a day or so to recover. Be understanding if they cancel plans by saying, "I'm just really tired." They'll probably already feel a bit guilty, so you can make them feel better about taking care of themselves by replying, "I totally understand! You need your rest, we'll reschedule!" An INFJ's need for space has nothing to do with how they feel about about you and your friendship. They need that alone time to continue being a great friend.

Be patient

INFJs are naturally private about their emotions. They don't like sharing too much of themselves and often find it hard to trust new friends. If you are just getting to know an INFJ, be patient. Don't push them to hard to be open and vulnerable. When they do express something personal, treat it with respect and kindness. Realize that sharing it is a significant step for the INFJ. The INFJ will know they are safe with you and they'll be more comfortable sharing in the future. The friendship will grow.

INFJs may still need time to express their emotions to people they do trust and know very well. This is because they just aren't used to being the vulnerable one; they're used to listening to other people's problems. Communicating their own takes practice, and it can sometimes be disorganized and rambly. Being a good friend in this situation includes letting the INFJ piece together their thoughts out loud without interrupting or jumping in with your own insights. Let them vent. They'll get there eventually.

Reflections/discussion questions

- Describe your ideal friend. Do you think it would be possible for a person to meet those standards?
- If you have trouble being vulnerable, why do you think that might be?
- You're not an INFJ, but you have an INFJ friend or family member: what specific things do you think might make them feel loved?

Chapter 5: INFJs In Love

There's nothing quite like an INFJ when it comes to love and romance. INFJs are drawn to the concept of soulmates and love that withstands any storm. They dream of fairy-tale romances and history's greatest love stories. Just like they have high expectations for friends, they have high standards for romantic partners. This means it can take a while for an INFJ to find someone. They want someone who can be their best friend *and* lover, and they strive to embody both those roles for their partner in return.

When an INFJ does find love, they are passionate and committed. People in relationships with INFJs are very lucky and will never want for attention. The INFJ tries to learn everything they can about their partner's interests and needs, and encourage them to follow their dreams. Whenever their partner has a bad day, an INFJ will instantly notice and jump in with some kind, encouraging words. INFJs also need that affirmation back from their partner. Since INFJs frequently feel misunderstood, they need their partner to accept and appreciate them.

Strengths

As an INFJ, you bring a lot of great things into romantic relationships. Thanks to your intuition, you can anticipate your partner's wants and needs, and decipher their moods without words. INFJs also dive right in to whatever their loved one is interested in, so they can share interests. This makes your partner feel really seen and understood. The last two strengths, commitment and encouragement, build very strong relationships where trust is never in doubt. Your partner will never worry about where you stand or if you believe in them.

INFJs read their partners like a book

We've talked a lot about how good INFJs are at reading people, including their non-verbal expressions. They can be so in-tune with others' emotions that it makes them appear psychic. An INFJ will apply that skill to their partner and since that relationship is so important to them, they'll direct a lot of their intuitive energy toward them. Whether it's anticipating how their partner will feel about something or choosing a gift, an INFJ will always know what to do or say. Their partner is like their favorite book; they know it front to back.

INFJs are invested in their partners' interests and needs

Partners of INFJs are consistently surprised by what the INFJ can remember about them. They might mention a story once about going camping with their family as a child and how much they loved it, and then a year later, their INFJ partner surprises them with a camping trip. That's because INFJs are very keen to share their partner's interests. They want to know everything about their hobbies and passions. When their partner reads a book or watches a movie and really loves it, the INFJ will want to read or watch it, too. Their partner loves basketball, so the INFJ will start watching games even when they aren't together, so they can talk about it later. An INFJ's partner will feel special, respected, and appreciated.

INFJs are fully-committed

Because of their high standards, it can take INFJs a bit longer to find a relationship they really believe in, but once they do, they love with their whole heart. They don't waffle or flake out. While INFJs can date casually, you'll rarely find them dating multiple people at once for very long. Once they find their soulmate connection, they'll drop the other romances and become laser-focused. Their partner will know they're loved, and that the INFJ plans to stick around for the long-term. INFJs want romances and marriages that last 50-60 years till death do us part.

INFJs encourage and inspire

INFJs encourage their partners just like they encourage their friends and family. When they sense negativity or discouragement, they'll be there with warm, supportive, and even inspiring encouragement. They know exactly what specific thing makes their partner feel better - a long hug without words, a pep talk, a special dessert, and so on - and they'll provide it. If you need to talk and vent, your INFJ partner will always be ready to listen. If you're struggling with an identity crisis or worried that you won't be able to fulfill your dreams, an INFJ will encourage you, build you up, and be supportive in whatever way you need. Partners of INFJs will have their morale boosted, their sense of self restored, and their strength to take on any challenge recharged.

Challenges

No love story is perfect and INFJs have their share of challenges as well as strengths. Many overlap with the challenges of maintaining friendships, though they can be amplified in a romantic partnership. Their high expectations can lead to disappointment, while an inability to set boundaries is exhausting and draining. INFJs also sometimes set too *many* boundaries with their own emotional vulnerability. Let's explore these challenges more in depth:

INFJs have high expectations

Having high standards for romantic relationships is not inherently a bad thing. In fact, it can actually protect you from a lot of bad romances and abuse, but if those expectations are unrealistically high, it can lead to disappointment. An INFJ might love someone, but become too focused on having a perfect, conflict-free fairy tale love that doesn't exist. You'll start to only notice what you dislike about the relationship and try to change your partner, who starts to feel like they'll never be good enough. A relationship like this is unhealthy and doesn't fulfill either person. It can also lead to frequent breakups for the INFJ, who leaves any relationship that doesn't match their unattainable ideal. You begin to believe you'll never find someone. Bitterness and regret starts to color your view of love, which is no way to live.

They have trouble setting boundaries

INFJs go all in with their romantic relationships, sometimes to the expense of their individuality. You want to always be there for your partner, meet their needs, and ensure their happiness. However, if your partner requires a lot of attention and starts to depend exclusively on you, it's draining. You start making too many emotional compromises like giving up your much-needed alone time. This strain can only continue for so long, and then you break down. You might even snap and become angry, only to become guilty afterwards. The other consequence is to withdraw without explanation, which can make your partner feel abandoned and insecure. If the your partner confronts you, there will be more guilt and more overextending. To maintain your own health and emotional strength as an INFJ, you need to set boundaries.

INFJs fear vulnerability

INFJs desire relationships where there are no secrets. They want intimate soul connections where both people can feel completely safe and loved. However, INFJs are also hesitant to share too much of themselves. They prefer to hear other peoples' stories and insecurities, and support them. When it comes to their own, INFJs are afraid to be too vulnerable. In romantic relationships, an equal share of vulnerability is crucial. Without that, your partner might believe you don't trust them or feel safe. They'll start to wonder why and become exhausted trying to prove themselves. Eventually, if the you don't let down your walls, the relationship might break down completely. Everyone loses.

Is there a perfect match for an INFJ?

Certain personality types get along better with others; does that apply to romance, too? Is there a perfect match for an INFJ? It depends on the individuals, of course. In general, however, INFJs can be happy with just about every personality as long as they share common values. Whether or not your partner is extroverted or introverted, or driven by thinking or feeling, doesn't matter as much as values like respect and commitment. That said, there are certain functions that make certain people better fits for an INFJ.

As an INFJ, you take the words of the 2003 Jewel song seriously: "Follow your heart/Your intuition/It will lead you in the right direction." Because that is your dominant function, you will do best with a partner who also has an intuitive function. Together, you'll share deep conversations, share stories, and unravel the complexities of one another's souls. Communication will be easier and more natural because you both can read non-verbals and pick up on subtle shifts in vocal tones. You'll both feel understood. There are two specific types with intuition that are great fits for INFJS: INTJs and ENTPs.

INTJs

These two personality types are very similar and when they first meet, they see themselves in the other person. They have an immediate, deep connection thanks to their shared intuition function and introversion. They're both relatively reserved and love deep conversations. An INFJ will be able to talk for hours about anything their heart desires - philosophy, art, science, spirituality - with an INTJ.

There's one key difference with these two - the "T" versus the "F" function. While an INFJ lives in a world of feelings, the INTJ is driven by logic and reason. They can help balance each other. An INFJ can become overwhelmed by their emotions. Their INTJ partner can help add anchor them back to reality with their logical, more structured thinking. They'll talk through problems with more objectivity.

On the other side, the INTJ can get too analytical and cut off from their emotion. INFJs can help them reconnect with that part of themselves and feel more passionately. These differences can sometimes cause conflict, especially if one or both people are unwilling to leave their comfort zones. They both have strong inner compasses and if they choose to follow them instead of compromising, the relationship won't work. If they are willing to be flexible, however, an INFJ and INTJ are a very healthy match.

ENTPs

ENTPs and INFJs share their "N," their intuitive function, and they are usually enjoy strong communication and understanding. They're also both creative-minded and geared toward abstract thinking and problem-solving. INFJS and ENTPS like to dream together.

These two personalities have contrasting traits, as well, and they can balance each other out. How, exactly? ENTPs have an *extroverted intuition* function, which means they are very open and more restless than the reserved, private INFJ. ENTPs can encourage openness and adventure in their INFJ partners. On the other side, INFJs can help ENTPS avoid their temptation for self-destruction and risk-prone restlessness. INFJS are a calming presence. There's also a contrast between the Feeling and Thinking functions; they support each other and can add balance in discussions and conflicts.

What INFJs can do to ensure happy relationships

Healthy, happy relationships involving INFJs are built to last. If you're an INFJ, what can you do to achieve your happy ending or improve your existing relationship? Self-care and clear communication are crucial, as is being able to adjust your expectations if they're sky-high and not based in reality. For those who are still looking for love, be patient and willing to socialize a bit more.

Follow your interests when looking for a partner

INFJs frequently have trouble finding romance because of their natural privacy, high expectations, and introversion. They aren't going to be hitting the bars and clubs, scouting for potential new partners, and they often cycle through shallow relationships when they don't feel a real connection. It can be frustrating and exhausting. What you can do is socialize with people who are more likely to think like you, or at least like the same things. Join a book club, take a class, or resolve to go to gatherings where you only know one person. Make it a goal to talk to at least 1-3 new people.

There are lots of resources like MeetUp where you can find groups catering to very specific interests. Be sure to exercise the appropriate amount of caution when meeting people you only know online, such as meeting in public places during the day, telling people where you're going, and so on.

Take care of yourself

When in a relationship, INFJs tend to focus on their partner's needs and wants at the expense of their own. This is especially true if their partner is extroverted and likes to go out a lot or hates being alone. You might sacrifice your need to recharge. This is disastrous for a relationship. Without alone time, you will eventually become too exhausted to maintain your composure. You might experience a breakdown and say things to your partner that you regret, or withdraw and leave them feeling neglected.

To ensure happiness in your romantic relationship, you *must* take care of yourself. Let your partner know that you don't want to go to that party; you need a few hours by yourself. When writing up your shared schedule, don't let them take over and fill it with activities if you know it will be too much for you. Be honest and open about your needs. If it's a healthy relationship, they'll understand.

Be clear and intentional in your communication

INFJs can read people's emotions even when they aren't spoken. However, most personalities can't do that, so an INFJ needs to be much clearer and intentional when expressing their feelings. This can be challenging since as you know, INFJs are private and dislike conflict. You might be hesitant to talk to your partner about something that bothers you because you're afraid they might feel hurt or even angry. Instead, you hope that they'll pick up on your body language and other non-verbals. However, they probably aren't able to do that, especially if you haven't been together for years and years. You'll feel misunderstood and disappointed.

The solution? Talk to them. Clearly explain what you're feeling without making them feel guilty about not picking up on your non-verbal expressions. Be willing to open up and be more vulnerable with them, even if it's hard. The relationship will be much stronger with improved communication.

<u>Be willing to adjust your expectations</u>

As an INFJ, you probably have pretty high expectations. You might not think you do, but if you find yourself frequently disappointed and believe you'll never find "true love," it might be time to take a closer look at your standards. When you first start dating someone, how do you expect them to act? Do you expect frequent text check-ins, deep conversations that last into the night, or a meet-the-parents date right away? How do you feel when that doesn't happen? Think about the person and if you are asking things of them that they might not be able to give. Also, have you actually talked to them about what you expect? They might be more than willing to meet your standards, but they just have no idea that you have them in the first place.

You don't have to give up *all* your expectations in a romantic relationship. In fact, you definitely should not, because those can prevent you from ending up with an ill-fitting or even abusive partner. However, think about your priorities - what's most essential to your happiness - and learn to relax your other standards a bit. Sure, it would be nice if your partner brought home flowers on Fridays or texted "I love you" every morning, but are those actions as important as sharing your spiritual beliefs? Or always being able to make you laugh when you feel sad? No relationship is perfect, despite what INFJs might aspire to, so learn to recognize what a healthy romance looks like in the real world.

What partners of INFJs can do

If you aren't an INFJ, you might be wondering what you can do to strengthen your romance with someone of this personality type. There are four actions that target an INFJ's strengths and weaknesses, so you are both affirming them and helping them expand their horizons. Let's take a closer look:

<u>Respect their space</u>

If you're an extrovert, you probably need a lot of stimulation. Even if you aren't, you might have fallen into a pattern where you prefer to be with your partner rather than totally alone. Whether you're an E or an I, maybe you've unconsciously started to expect your partner to always be available. This doesn't work for

INFJs. They need time by themselves where they don't have to think about other people, even you. Because of their intuition and feeling functions, they're designed to always be reading whoever is around them, and striving to make them happy. If you're always with them, they never get a chance to turn that part off. They need to recharge.

Respect your partner's need for space. You don't necessarily have to anticipate when they need it (though that never hurts), but be completely accepting when they express that need. They might feel guilty, so be sure to assure them that you understand and aren't taking it as a personal insult. Your INFJ partner loves you with their whole heart; their need for space doesn't mean that's changed. In fact, getting a break means they can keep loving you in a healthy, fulfilling way. It benefits both of you.

Affirm their individuality

INFJs often feel misunderstood and isolated from the rest of society. Many have trouble making deep connections, and because others don't usually possess the INFJ's level of compassion and awareness of emotions, they frequently feel underappreciated or neglected. They start to wonder if it would be better if they were different; maybe if they didn't talk about their quirky interests as much or were more outgoing, they would have more friends. As their partner, it's your job to love them for who they are, and let them know.

When they want to talk, let them talk, even if the topic seems random. Be engaged, or the INFJ will start to wonder if they're boring you. If you feel like you don't know about about the subject, take it upon yourself to do some independent research. This will make your partner feel special and appreciated; they go to a lot of effort to share your interests, you can do the same for them. In addition to deep conversations, INFJs also like to dream big. Depending on your personality type, you might be tempted to "tell it like it is" and rain on their parade a little. Resist. INFJs are idealistists, but they're also strong-willed enough to actually see things through to the end. If they feel like you believe in them, there's very little they can't do.

Encourage adventure

INFJs are introverts, but that doesn't mean they don't love trying new things. They're big fans of planned spontaneity, which means trying something new and adventurous, but getting a head's up about it. For example, they would not love being told, "Hey, get in the car, we're going skydiving!" but if you asked, "How would you like to try skydiving sometime this year?" they're much more likely to be totally on board. INFJs can expand their horizons with partners who encourage them to live life to the fullest. What that looks like exactly and how adventurous things get depends on the couple. In general, INFJs do very well with romantic partners who inspire them to get out of their heads, so don't be afraid to push a little.

Take care of yourself

INFJs are natural caregivers and counselors. They can sense when you've had a bad day and are always there to provide comfort. You might start to depend on them to lift your mood. The problem? That isn't the INFJ's job. You need to take responsibility for your own happiness and not lean exclusively on your partner. INFJs are a bit like emotional sponges; they absorb the feelings of those around them, especially their romantic partner. If you go to them every time you feel sad or angry, they'll feel dragged down. They probably won't say anything, either, because they have such a strong desire to help.

It's up to you to take care of yourself. This doesn't mean bottling up your emotions and never being vulnerable with your partner. You should still talk to them about your feelings. However, instead of waiting for them to change your mood or your view on a hard situation, do a little internal work of your own. Be your own encourager. Your partner will feel better about your emotional state and won't feel the need to "fix" things. They will be able to share in the moment with you without needing to step into their therapist role. You can be emotional equals.

How does an INFJ recover from a breakup?

What happens when a romantic relationship doesn't work out? INFJs are deeply-affected by breakups, because they want to believe in forever. Splitting from a partner can feel like the end of the world, and an INFJ should allow themselves to heal, process, and nurture trusting relationships with friends.

Accept that healing takes time

Healing isn't linear and it's different for everyone. It isn't so much about how long a relationship lasted, but more about how much energy you put into it. Ending an intense relationship that lasted six months can feel like a major event, and it should be treated as such. Respect your emotions and accept that healing will take time. Don't let society dictate how long your process should take or what it should look like. If you feel misunderstood by your friends and family, consider seeing a therapist. The right one will provide a judgement-free environment where you can vent and receive healthy coping techniques.

Invest in people you trust

When an INFJ breaks up with their significant other, their first instinct (usually) is to crawl in a ball and stay in bed. This alone time is necessary for internal processing, but it can easily go too far and become isolating. INFJs, like all people, are built for community. Feeling connected and loved is truly healing and will strengthen your confidence in yourself and others. Take shelter in the people you trust the most. Take the energy you used for your ended relationship and put it into your friends and family. Be clear with them about what you need, too, since you may have friends who want to give you advice when all you want is to vent. They may not be able to pick up on this desire from your non-verbals if they don't have an intuitive function. Communicating intentionally and clearly ensures you get the support you need.

Push yourself a little

As we mentioned before, INFJs will probably want to just be alone following a breakup. They guard their emotions and vulnerability, and if they don't feel completely confident in their friendships or family, they won't go to them for support. Depending on the circumstances of the breakup, an INFJ might feel like they can't trust anyone anymore. If you're feeling this way, reconsider your beliefs. Do you truly not have anyone in your life you can trust? Or are you using that as a excuse to not open up emotionally? Healing can be painful at times, but it's worth it.

Following a breakup, you should also push yourself out of the house and out of your own head. Yes, you'll need to process, but that can get overwhelming and you'll start to go around in circles. Get outside, go for a walk with the dog. Meet a friend for coffee or a movie, if you don't want to talk. If you find yourself at home alone most nights, stewing in your emotions, push yourself to break the routine.

Reflections/discussion questions

- Describe your ideal partner. Does it seem realistic? What traits are most important?
- If you tend to lose yourself in a romantic relationship, what are some specific

things you could do to set boundaries
and perform more self-care?

- You aren't an INFJ, but you love one:
list some specific ways you can let them
know how much they mean to you.

Chapter 6: INFJs and Parenting

What are INFJs like as parents? They don't take the role on lightly, that's for sure. At their best, INFJs are very nurturing and warm parents who encourage their kids to follow their dreams. The relationship is usually very close and strong; the child feels assured that their parent will always be there for them, no matter what. They aren't afraid of expressing whatever emotion they're feeling. If the INFJ has multiple kids, they're usually very good at deciphering how each one feels, thanks to their intuition, and able to empathize. The child feels seen and understood, which is essential for their confidence and sense of self.

INFJs pour a lot of energy into passing on wisdom and values to their children, and often worry about being a good enough role model. This can lead to some self-doubt about their fitness as a parent, which in turn translates into the need to control. INFJ parents are often strict and pressure their kids into sharing their values. A controlling INFJ is very uncomfortable with their kids making mistakes; in an effort to protect them, they can become too dominating.

Strengths

INFJs have a lot of traits that make them great parents. They seek to understand and respect their kids, and build them up. If you are kind, empathetic, and forgiving, you have all the makings of a parent who will nurture and encourage your children into a self-assured, compassionate adult.

INFJs strive to understand their kids

We all had parents or some kind of parental figure in your lives, and odds are, what we desired most from them was understanding. This is what every person seeks in their relationships. The need to feel *seen* and respected, to be acknowledged as an individual with value, is what unites us all as human beings. If you're an INFJ, the rarest and most misunderstood personality type, you probably work very hard to ensure your kids have this sense of self. With your intuitive function, you are able to read your child's emotions and respond in a way that shows the kid those emotions are respected. The INFJ parent wants their kid to know they are not alone.

When raised with respect and understanding, children grow up self-assured with a healthy, inner sense of their own value. They are less likely to depend on others for validation and less susceptible to societal pressure. They will be their own person.

INFJs are compassionate and forgiving

We've talked a lot about how INFJs are naturally very kind and warm. They absorb the emotions of those around them in a truly empathetic way, and are great listeners. When these traits are present in the parent role, INFJs encourage honesty and vulnerability without the fear of reprisal. While you may remember being scared to tell your parent(s) you failed a math test, kids of compassionate and forgiving INFJs won't be. They won't think, "My dad/mom is going to kill me." When a kid is afraid of their parent, they will bottle up emotions they believe are "bad." They won't share when they've done something wrong or even destructive, which can have long-term negative consequences.

However, when an INFJ parent establishes a precedent of forgiveness and empathy, kids feel very comfortable sharing without fear. Even if they've done something wrong or they're embarrassed about a feeling or behavior, the child is confident that their parent will respond with forgiveness and encouragement. This can prevent destructive and tragic behaviors (like addictions), while at the very least, it builds a stronger bond between you and your child.

INFJs encourage strong values

INFJs are also known as Advocates and Counselors. We've discussed what those mean in earlier chapters, but as a refresher, it means that INFJs are driven by a desire to make the world a better place and to help others. As parents, INFJs instill these goals in their kids. According to the website 16Personalities, the "highest goal" for an INFJ is that their child's beliefs lead to a cause that improves society. As an INFJ, you want your kids to be compassionate and selfless. The definition of "success" for you probably isn't tied to money or status. When your kid stands up for someone being bullied, joins a college advocate group, or gets a job at a non-profit, you're filled with pride.

Challenges

INFJs can be very caring, supportive parents who treat their kids as individuals who deserve respect, but there are still challenges that tend to manifest in this personality type. The two most notable ones: high expectations and emotional burnout. These are present in other types of relationships, as well, so it makes sense that they apply to the parent-child relationship, too.

An INFJ's high expectations can be projected unto a child

INFJs have high standards for their friends, significant others, and themselves. Unfortunately, this weakness can carry over to their kids to an unhealthy degree. It can overwhelm your more compassionate and understanding traits, so your kid feels inadequate. Feeling like they'll never be good enough is extremely damaging and can lead to unhealthy perfectionism or dangerous rebellion.

A child who feels like they aren't meeting their parents' expectations often exhausts them trying to get there. They become perfectionists to a fault, always critiquing themselves, and harboring very low self-esteem. They stop being vulnerable with their parents or others, repress emotions they see as "bad," and never seek help. Eventually, they burn out or have a full-on breakdown, which makes them feel even worse. On the other hand, they might respond to sky-high expectations by rebelling. "Why even try?" they say to themselves, and act out in ways they know their parent will hate, even if it's self-destructive. An INFJ's child may even alternate between seeking perfection and giving up. Whatever road they take, their relationship with their parent(s) will be rocky and exhausting. Until they believe they are enough in their parents' eyes, they'll struggle.

<u>Parenting can be exhausting for an INFJ</u>

In friendships and romantic relationships, INFJs need their space. However, when it comes to parenting, that's much harder to find. Kids need a lot of attention, and as a parent, an INFJ always wants to provide that. They can become too accommodating at the expense of their own sanity. This leads to burnout. If you're an INFJ and a parent, you are probably familiar with your "breaking point," or the realization that you can't handle anymore. Every personality type has one, actually, but types like INFJs who really need time to recharge may feel it more keenly. If you're fortunate enough to have the support from a partner or other relationships, you can hand off your kid(s) and get some alone time.

Sadly, many INFJs aren't able to do this because of their circumstances. More often than not, however, it's because they don't want to ask for help. INFJs don't like being vulnerable, and admitting that parenting is taking too much out of them might bring out feelings of guilt and inadequacy. If they ignore their internal warning system, their parenting strengthens will weaken and it can damage the parent-child relationship.

How INFJS can be better parents

When it comes to improving the parent-child relationship, there are two things that an INFJ can do that also apply to every other relationship: adjusting expectations and making room for self-care. The third tip is exclusive to parenting, however, and might be tricky: being a parent, not a friend. Keep reading to the end of this section to find out what that means exactly.

Adjust expectations

Everyone thinks they know what's best for their kid. INFJs have high standards and their kids won't always be able to meet them. Instead of focusing on how your kid can improve and trying to mold them into the perfect son or daughter, take a look at your expectations. If you know you tend to expect a lot from friends, family, and/or your partner, odds are you're doing the same thing with your children, too. Spend some time prioritizing what you want from your kids and what you can let go. Preventing habits that are dangerous should obviously take priority over everything else. Expecting your kid to get home at a certain time on the weekends will probably be more important than cutting back on time playing video games. Choose what you want to go to bat for and maybe relax some other rules.

Take care of self

It's necessary to take breaks, even from parenting. Resting and recharging allow you to be the best parent possible. When your kids are young and need more attention, be intentional about fostering a trusted community of babysitters, so you can get a night off every few weeks or how ever often you need. As kids age, their needs change, but parenting can still be exhausting. Consider family therapy if it seems like you're always fighting with your kids, or therapy just for yourself if you need a safe space to vent and process. When you become a parent, you don't stop being an individual with your own needs. Remember self-care.

Be a parent, not a friend

Because of their natural empathy, INFJs will easily relate to their kids. That can go too far at times. Maybe you'll avoid establishing rules because you don't want to appear strict, or you keep silent when you spot a behavior you don't believe is healthy because you don't want to be judgemental. These are classic examples of an INFJ parent trying to be their kids' friend and not a parent. Lots of kids need the structure and guidance only a parent can provide. Without it, they'll feel lost or engage in reckless behaviors. One of the best things an INFJ can remember is that the parent-child relationship isn't the same as a friendship. The specific rules and boundaries depend on you and how many rules and structures your child needs.

What is it like to be the parent of an INFJ?

Not an INFJ, but believe one or more of your kids might be? How do you adjust your child-rearing style to be the best parent possible to them? Here are three tips:

Help them express their emotions in a healthy way

As they age, INFJ kids grow into their intuition and feeling function. They become deeply affected by the emotions of others and often unsure about what to do. They'll be tempted to stay quiet and stew, which can be exhausting and even lead to depression and/or anxiety. Help them learn to express their emotions in a healthy way by being available to talk and encouraging vulnerability. Be the safe space they need to open up without fear of judgement. Fine-tune your own ability to read their emotions and check in, so they know you want you to listen. INFJs don't always feel like talking, so observe how they express their creativity and encourage it. Give them a journal, a set of paints, or sheet music. They'll channel their emotions into creating something beautiful, and in the process, they will most likely be ready to have a conversation.

Be sensitive of their space and need for solitude

INFJs need alone time, so don't be surprised when your INFJ kid retreats to their room after school or isn't excited about hanging out in large groups. Young INFJ kids will also be sensitive to loud noises, bright lights, and other external stimulation, so pay attention to how they react. They might start to act out in a desperate attempt to tell you something is off, so be patient and don't get angry with them. There's nothing wrong with them and they shouldn't be pressured to change.

Give INFJ kids their space. If you start to worry that perhaps they're spending *too* much time alone and you think they might be depressed, talk to them. Get the full story. Avoid pulling them into social situations where they'll be uncomfortable and overwhelmed by too much external stimulation. They'll feel misunderstood and even more alone, which will make any existing depression much worse.

Help them learn to set boundaries

Boundary-setting is one of the hardest things for INFJs to do. As a parent, you will be doing your child a great service by helping them learn how when they are young. Keep an eye on the friends who come into their life. Are you spotting any toxic or even abusive relationships? Talk to your kid about their friends. If your kid feels comfortable being vulnerable and sharing what they really feel, you'll be able to tell if these are fulfilling or one-sided friendships. Are they making excuses for certain behaviors? In a non-judgemental, loving way, let your kid know that it's okay to step back from certain friendships and that their own emotional state is a priority, too.

Be cautious about taking matters into your own hands and cutting them off from people (unless their safety is at risk), because this could lead to your kid continuing a friendship or relationship behind your back. You want them to understand what's going on and be the one to make the tough choices. When they get older, you won't be the one deciding who they spend time with, but if you've taught them self-assurance and the ability to draw lines, they will be much better at setting boundaries.

Reflections/discussion questions

- What does parenthood mean to you? What is the most rewarding part, and what is the most challenging?

- Write down all the things you expect from your child. How many of them are being met? If there ratio is really skewed, think about why and if your expectations are too high.
- You're the parent of an INFJ: think about specific ways you can connect with them and affirm them as individuals.

Conclusion

Built from theories by Carl Jung, Katharine Briggs, and Isabel Meyers, the Meyers-Briggs Indicator reveals a lot about personalities and why all of us are the way we were. INFJs, who are introverted, iNtuitive, feeling, and judging, are the rarest type and often misunderstood. In this book, we explored how the INFJ breaks down into Dominant, Auxiliary, Tertiary, and Inferior functions. If you are an INFJ, you possess a keen introverted intuition that many people find psychic, and an extroverted feeling that draws others to you. You are compassionate, considerate, and may even appear extroverted. INFJs also possess an introverted thinking function, and their weakest function, extraverted sensing, results in sensitivity to loud noises, crowds, and other sensory stimuli.

How do these traits manifest in life's different arenas, like work, friendships, romantic relationships, and parenting? Through this book's six chapters, you learned that INFJs need alone time to process, a safe space to vent, and a sense of purpose. In every type of relationship, INFJs are known for their warmth and encouragement, but they often have high expectations that can cause division and pain. INFJs pour their whole heart into something, whether it's a job or a friendship, so they often need breaks and positive affirmation. They strongly dislike conflict, which can prevent petty arguments, but cause issues when tough decisions or tough love is the best option.

The Meyers-Briggs Indicator isn't the final word on your personality, but it provides an excellent foundation for better understanding. Continue to do research and seek out resources on the INFJ type to learn more, and spend time reflecting on how you can lean into your strengths. Through all your experiences, remember this: no matter what your personality type and the challenges that come with it, you are a unique human being worthy of love and respect.

67392140R00059

Made in the USA
Columbia, SC
26 July 2019